Y0-AFI-833

DAMASCUS, ATLANTIS
selected poems

Marie Silkeberg

DAMASCUS, ATLANTIS
selected poems

Fountaindale Public Library District
300 W. Briarcliff Rd.
Bolingbrook, IL 60440

translated by
Kelsi Vanada

© 2021 by Marie Silkeberg
translation © 2020 Kelsi Vanada

ISBN: 9781949597110
Library of Congress Control Number: 2020950610

All rights reserved.

contains poems from:
Till Damaskus, Albert Bonniers Förlag, 2014 (together with Ghayath Almadhoun)
Atlantis, Albert Bonniers Förlag, 2017

images from these films:
The City © Marie Silkeberg & Ghayath Almadhoun, 2012
Snow © Marie Silkeberg & Ghayath Almadhoun, 2015

published by

Terra Nova Press
NEWARK   CALLICOON   MATSALU

Publisher: David Rothenberg
Editor-in-Chief: Evan Eisenberg
Translator: Kelsi Vanada
Designer: Bernhard Wöstheinrich

set in Adobe Garamond Pro, AT Rotis Sans Serif and Montserrat

The cost of this translation was defrayed by a subsidy
from the Swedish Arts Council, gratefully acknowledged.

Additional funding came from the Längman Culture Foundation,
also gratefully acknowledged.

printed by Tallinn Book Printers, Tallinn Estonia

www.terranovapress.com
Distributed by the MIT Press, Cambridge, Massachusetts and London, England

Table of Contents

from **Seventh Gate | The Wave**

watch the cat looking at me while it purrs on his arm. his sleeping face. world-stillness. in August heat. a whole life. the temperature he says caressing my shoulders. the same. straight roads. canals. four rivers. five bridges. bathed our feet in the canal. his feet got covered in rust. opened my eyes. to see his face. dreamed. amber tears from the amber eyes. the brief moment I fell asleep. white painting. red bridge. the blue one. the light from the river. 2017 he says. next wave. the centennial. it will be violent he says. *the one. the last.* figure. white mountain. whispering to the mountain. thousand voices. mountain, angel. the mountain of the dead. new dreams. chainless. Field of Mars. as if the years were pouring over. through the halls. like scraps. unwanted matter. emptied. the empty places. one morning. in sun. heat. music through the night. from the neighbors below. magnified face. in sleep. *touch and touch me not.* the first day. a fractal. the first over the many. days. *I lost my sense.* it was people. not the killing machine. people beating each other up. ratting on others. torturing. to get an apartment for instance he says. the grid of the streets. always corner apartments he says. a cross. the streets. revolutionary youth. community. nonviolence. *raskol.* splitting. through the layers. a few moments of clarity he says. in the park. before the murder. to open the wrong door. to find piles of corpses. the blue color. naming the crime. the guilt. gulls. from the Neva. over the Neva. he cried. an opening between the worlds. in the kitchen. the dream. transversal. major renovation of the square. where a church was blown up long ago to build an entrance to the metro. the new one. deep. seven minutes. ten. to reach the platform. a whole naked line. hipbone. sex. *it will be violent.* the wave. continue he says on the stairs. felt the vibrations when the heavy trucks drove over the highest point. where the bridge is drawn. at night. the feline. the third day. wake up. and want nothing more. than being close to. the pronoun of night. sought the edge of the house against the sky. the silhouette. the intersection. the low. long. horizon line. nuclear submarines. dockyard. just one drop of the water. unreachable opening. to the sea. transparent sleep. shadows on the sidewalk. how they are traced. sun's rays. the bodies. the feather-weight image. hunger. heat. toward evening. the market. piles of dill. coriander. giant radishes. chili. dairy products. the kitchen. the cat. white. Oriental breed. settles onto my knee. they look at each other. outside the market. the shade's coolness. Pravdy Ulitsa. a mild breeze. out of nowhere. the breeze that sweeps. coolness in August. his voice. the park. do you remember. I do. the ground. the names of the fishes. particles swirl in the light. dense tree canopy. balustrade. nocturnal streets. a boat at high speed. breaks up the reflections. the orange reflections. love is an ocean she sings. a mystery. how old is the girl. a whole

life. it's burning, L writes. just kidding a second later. desire he intones. like no one else. Aleppo. the destruction. mirrored in his eyes. images from the market. the old city. ruins. gravel. through the day. the dream. the fragrance. aircraft drawing contrails above the cathedral. they have time enough to call Aleppo he says. from Damascus. when they see the missiles. they have eight minutes. seven signals. the dose

from **The Cities**

in reverse. sonic textures. two boys went home from the baker's. crossing the paving stones. the puddles. systematic blasting. by hand. house by house. went astray. went along the canal. the Spree. the construction site. castle. cathedral. a large open square. snow sculptures. mirrorcubes. every time I try to imagine the city I see Sergel's Torg fronting me. the black and white plaza. the snow crystals outside the central station. like a blocking out. volcano. volcanic ash. bashful Pompeii. cats in Istanbul. junction. a glimpse of the Bosporus. je t'interpelle dans la nuit. Anatolia. seagulls angle. two by two. across the sky. the courtyard. it trickles down into the alley. the passage. the sun through the clouds. awnings. closed eyes. the choice not to travel. yet. maybe I was hallucinating he says but it seems you've already told me that. at the gates. started bleeding freely. simultaneously from all wounds. huge cargo ships went toward the strait. the opening. disappeared out to sea. two sides. the alley. the courtyard. of the face. strange amalgam. freeze. I threw all my coins into the tollbooth. emptied my pockets. for a prayer never to have to return again. I see their faces are so alike. in some angle of consciousness. over the bridge. felt it was irremediable. the loss. the departure. the first. the second. I don't know. I'll try to feel pain throughout the whole journey he says. the abyss I answer. it has started to slide. dark alley. a cat rubs against my leg. a man with both legs amputated at the kneecaps is moving across the sunlit sidewalk. a heavily loaded truck gets stuck in the broken street. sways. *a phrase with two memories*. the bottles clink. *open so to speak*. until they are wholly still. *on both sides*. således udfriet. city glittering. in sunset search after eros a trial of the heart. the membranes. if morning could arrive. sleep. a dimension of freedom. somewhere dogs bark. in the night. the anxiety like an ache. a dizziness in the body. a state of shock. kicks. kicks. against the fetal membranes. streetlight-lit greenery. the long-eared owl in the awakening city. the searching gaze. over the facades. boulevards. the many cars. among lilacs and chestnuts. pollution. traces of bullet holes in the house walls. no wind at night. stray dogs. a pack. out of sight. the earthquake. Vrancea. six point five on the Richter scale she says. the replica. I placed myself in the doorway she says. the house swayed. all the concrete. the books fell off the shelf. plates cups glasses. the piano she says. like a black monster slowly moving across the floor. the last books fell. body's sensors. the hair stood up on my neck. in that moment I could have strangled someone she says. out of terror. in that moment I knew I could kill. winter morning stillness. a flashing string of images. comprehensions. in the borderland. beyond the border. Stalin Square. the victims of the famine. a black dog in darkening mist. the poorly lit city. in haze. trembling exhaust light. the voice that speaks. has spoken. nourishment. across continents. pazhalsta. a woman with her child. at the crossing. the baby totally silent. cried silently. in reluctant light. the white room. I shudder every time I hear it she says. the tragedy of being a human being. after being a woman. Ukrainian. the doubling in the labyrinth. to enter darkness. change places. be left behind. become one of them. unable to be translated back. at the very threshold of the station. birth. second birth. experiencing what has not been gone through. the squinting glance. the double. to embrace. life. death. winter shadow. black or white magic. each reconstruction a loss. an erasure of erasure. it started happening in my own life she says. Andrea's Slope. acacias. agile and burning. fire smoke in the December chill. gray military coats displayed on the fence. a line of men raking leaves on the hillside. reluctant dawn light. white church. white patterned synthetic curtains. the quietude of the cobblestone streets. silence in the subway tunnels. despite the crowd of people. breath like a cloud over her frozen fingers. pork lard. the taste. smell. a strange perfume in the orange soap. revenge. torture. transition period. no end of history. no end of geography she says. during landing. archipelago in a bleeding sunset. with incredible speed the sun sinks at the brink

heat from hurricanes. or air currents. while oil flows over the forehead. along the hair. an image of the quay at the city hall. the view from Katarina Street. like a photograph. in blue twilight. flashes. like a photograph taken. in sleep. through sleep. in sleep's onset. still image. Scandic Hotel. the lights. the lights reflected in water. Japanese garden. when I turned the corner after seeing its patterns. microcosm. a monk sat next to them singing a few words in Swedish. the running water. the flowing oil. the sound of running water. over the forehead. streaming heat from left to right. along the hairline. a heaviness in the hair. as if it were longer. reached farther. with one foot bare in the snow. land conquest. December second. turns to night. snowfall. I turn around. three men in black winter coats. the new-fallen snow. first tracks. music through the speakers. blaring music. otherwise wholly quiet. a jogging man passes by. the next second I'm not sure I wasn't dreaming. an electric cross illuminated by hundreds of tiny light bulbs. shines over the hillside. the other side. the ustorious night. an elusive child. gray snow. wrought iron. balconies. entire houses gutted. emptied. ice-blue. ice-green. color. fallen plaster. the crown of his head in my hand in the early morning. in the slow dawn light. phantoms of Europe. falling snow. snow crystals. monumental crap as aesthetic objects. I couldn't imagine the creative crisis was so deep. I heard her say. a photographic reconstruction of a flight through a city. a large star in the shape of a lance lit up in the west. from the fifteenth floor of Hotel Moscow. *breathing is darker.* famine victims. a void. where the stomach should have been. *and the medicine of night brings more hope.* at the site where the church once stood. until it was blown to pieces. cracks open. hear her say his name. many times. talking about food. grocers. an evening by the water. fish. many people. rushed through the streets. went over the bridge. up in the tower. saw the whole city from the highpoint. people gathering in the square. flocking to it. the lights. strong sensation of light. the individual. the community. the labyrinth. the nightmare. the event. handprint. I stood totally motionless in the blazing light. the women's line. vendor of water. coffee. cigarettes. conversion. the voice. of the people. counterforces. want. a drought. a taste of sand. sand in the mouth. fearless. sunlight. electrical shock to the senses. widening aperture. light intake

legitimacy. fear. the heart at the ruptured street. hear the sounds. the language. the brink. bolting event sequence. *perfect chance. change.* love's angle. knowledge's. dark corridors. clear glass. hard. at violence's crossing-point. violent movement. flight. struggle. the streets ended. had the wrong numbers. names. in some alley. with many birds in the spaces between the rooftops. the well. cats. in sunshine. one with an eye shut. peers. pregnant. the other black. the alley. it bleeds. in the veins. out of the body. construction workers. carry building materials under the curtain. abundant. *deeper. risk. rich. soil.* the up-and-down heads. on the side. Medusa's. underwater. the opening. Jason's route. large cargo ships slowly disappear into the mist. haze. sleek pigeons on the rooftops. a flock of white storks. across the bridge. a heron. in the silence of life. high rooms. running water. the sound of running water. life. love. bleeding through the veins. jump. jump. they shouted. in the silence of life. stared out over the Bosporus in the gray cold. hungover. barely awake. drank coffee. texted. went past fish restaurants by boat to the Anatolian side. under Galata Bridge. cold from the water. looked out over it. illuminated mosques. saw the muezzin through the open minaret door. the immense force. the force amassment. in silence. the voice of another muezzin in it. when I came to Sweden he says. after a long flight. where he remained hidden for eight months inside the country. before getting out. always had a gun with him in the bathroom. the first apartment. he says. in May. no blinds. hardly anything there. it was light until eleven at night. I didn't understand anything he says. how it could be so bright. so long. the central station. the snow crystals. the arrival. the dry cold. first time. first memory. how it's inscribed. as a second nature. inside. pain's abyss. having drilled down deep enough. or not deep enough. Basilica Cistern. Medusa's two heads. up and down. on the side. innermost. among the pillars. high stakes. the navel stone. marble disc in the high room. the hot surface. the naked body. the two faces. sides. another protest marches slowly through the streets. the barren sand scenery unfolds. there's blood on the streets now he says

Saint-Ouen | Stalingrad

Rashomon. The Demon's Gate you say.

I understood that it had opened.

Only a few more seconds. And it would be opened wide.

Time would stratify.

It snowed. The first snow fell.

On the metro you sit next to a man and a woman.

The woman starts talking.

You don't hear the first part.

Whether it was about her daughter.

Or someone else.

The man answers her.

Society will never help you.

Be happy you married me. Because I'm outside society.

She looks down.

As if he'd just hit her.

You get up when the metro stops and walk out the doors.

You win he calls to say.

You win nothing.

You took the elevator down into the cavern.

Seventy meters underground.

No phone signal.

You saw the white chairs.

The hole in the middle of the room.

Where the reactor had been removed.

The walls were covered in numbers written in chalk.

It resembled a tomb.

The white chairs.

fugue state

The chalky writing.

When a woman freed herself from the crowd you followed her.

Took the elevator up.

Went out onto the snow-filled street.

I need help he said.

With what you asked.

You see he said.

I need help.

The only thing you wanted was to sleep for a whole night.

You heard the birds.

Walked in the early morning.

Saw the gray sky.

The dry streets.

As far as the eye can see you thought.

Armed soldiers outside the school.

It will happen again he says.

You pass by a school. See the lit-up classrooms.

Empty that late in the afternoon.

Camps built and torn down.

People being moved he says.

Bon soir a man says on the street when you pass by him.

He stood at a doorway.

Bon soir you whispered back.

Looking down at the cobblestones.

Didn't want to turn the light on when you entered.

To let him know where you lived.

You moved in the darkness.

Fell asleep wondering.

Who to call if something happened.

do you see the man sitting in that car he asks

pointing toward a fenced-in area under the subway bridge

he sits there the whole day just guarding the evacuated space

You went to Porte de Clignancourt.

Got lost on your way from the metro.

you watch a man packing stuff up at closing time

taking off a mannequin's clothes

loosening its legs

in the setting sun

now they're running toward it from it you think

They don't even see them he says.

You're not allowed to talk about racism.

It doesn't exist.

No statistics.

Fifty-seven people sleep here on the street he says.

After they were thrown out of a house slated for renovation.

Half of them have no papers.

They're just lying right in the street.

Go to work in the morning.

Come back in the evening.

state of emergency

they can arrest people for ninety-six hours

he says next to nothing on the phone

we're all tapped he says

An area. A border.

The ring road.

it's totally irrelevant what you say

he says

everyone has to become poor

no one should be integrated

I'm against development

if they want to get out of poverty wouldn't you respect that you ask

you've also benefited from white privilege your entire life

You walked all the way down to the river.

In the light of the day.

why didn't you call he asks

it was late you say

you were far away

the globe is small he says

I was awake

The claustrophobic scenography. The drowned child.

The first stone image.

Scene image.

A child sliding down a staircase that looks like wooden sticks.

Vanishes between them. In dim blue light. The child in the aquarium.

The singing woman. The screaming one.

The stage. The aquarium. Filling with water.

A large shape.

Death-anxiety invades you.

During the performance.

Fear that death will be cold.

A slow deterioration.

The wounds and the water.

you have many things I don't you say

like what?

the Arabic language for instance

I can teach you

'ana

I am

'anti

you are

You remember watching a TV series with no resolution in wintertime.

Only an awakening of the dead. Who wanted to take revenge. On the living.

Their attempts at life.

You wait in the middle of the middle row for the play to finish.

For you to get out.

What do you find in poverty you ask.

Rage he answers.

You moved together from somewhere in the 3rd arrondissement.

Through the city.

Out of it. Past Gare du Nord.

Went under a low bridge.

Past a box that was sealed shut.

White cardboard.

About half a meter high.

Inside someone lay sleeping.

What kind of sleep you were thinking.

What is it to undertake such a sleep.

only two degrees tonight

it hailed

snowed

You came to a camp under another bridge.

A man sat by a fire.

He stretched out his hand. Greeting.

The man took it.

Drunk.

You walk by the place where the big camp once was situated.

Under a bridge by the ring road.

After the evacuation it had been blocked with concrete pillars.

The people were chased away.

Inside the tunnel the concrete pillars now lay crushed and scattered.

the police will soon evacuate the camp we're told

we have to do it tonight he says

more and more keep coming

there are over five hundred people there now

He gives coins to a man.

People are crazy he says.

Refuses to sit down under the heaters.

The warmth from the infrared and the patio heaters.

How can they sit outside in t-shirts in the middle of winter he says.

Everyone is living like it's the last days.

you go into a Somali restaurant to eat

the people from the camp seem to be charging their phones there

a net of cords lies over the narrow table

The slowly changing camera angles.

From above. Below. Rotations in the air.

Film with no main characters.

Extras.

we were fighting every ten minutes in the camp he says

As if the angles incisively delineated the feeling you think.

The border.

The road.

The landscape filled with pain.

As if watched by the olive trees.

I saw your brothers

your compatriots you think

I am happy if you are he writes

you're lying you answer

but I appreciate the intention

You thought about hybrid cities.

The violent wall.

Walls.

It's not illegal to occupy he says
ten percent of all the buildings in Paris stand empty

then why are they kept back you ask
to hold those down who are here already

Low tents stood behind the line of people.
A camp.
Smoke. Steam.
From the food in the cold.
The breath of the people waiting.
Coming from the north of Africa.
Or further south.
Françafrique.
The colonies.
In what can no longer be called a city.

aren't you exposing them to danger you ask
don't you think it looks like they're exposed to danger
already

Because cities are always uncontrollable growths he says.

Uncontrollable encounters.

Hazy transitions between life and death.

how long did you live in the camp you ask inside the occupied building

too long

Maybe they don't exist anymore in the cities.

The wealthy cities.

what kind of country is this that lets us sleep on the streets

not even blankets we're given

against the winter cold

Only the denial. The masking. The economic expansion.

The police force's.

Demolitions of the Roma's camps.

The patience with which they are built just a few kilometers further away.

To let the children continue at the same school.

I abandoned you he says

inhales

sorry

You looked out at the trees in the yard.

White houses.

Street sweepers cleaning the streets.

looks hot he writes

big meeting at Stalingrad

we might move tonight

She shows you a book whose images open like doors.

Further and further into the prison.

Previously a monastery.

Tells you about three trials.

The objects.

Of the prisoners and the judges.

What is your main concern you ask.

The crime or justice.

Justice she answers.

Hands

today I made the animation with a gun on one fingernail and it was shooting - - - - - -

even now. ghost. host. clear as crystal. several white sheets of cloth. seldom. a kind of erotic relation of resistance and abandonment. that was no ghost coming up the stairs. without wings. formulas for pathos. with the outside serving as soul. interpreted the oracle too boundlessly. an I with an insatiable appetite for the non-I. what's hiding there. in time. that space cannot lay bare. these weird flashbacks. not even the circle *tomorrow the technical specialist will come and at 8 I go to Moscow*

parallel texts. montage's edges

the main thing is the rhythm of glimmer with sound (your voice, old vinyl, noise of the city, et cetera) the letters on hands and faces violent blow-ups. dilated pupil. fall asleep in a few microseconds. as if the brain switched off. in long English sentences. for the first time. the first hand. sight. crowding images. at civilization's lock. to sleep in the holes beneath the buildings. keep moving. you know all this. no. I don't know. the little hole where it enters. the exit point where it sunders the skull. the pointing hand. the body across the street. a gray heap. if you run zigzag. maybe. the movement. one of a kind. one kind. it's snowing. big flakes. in each note. her voice. not the animal's. not the street's. shards of glass. wakefulness in the night. his night. that everything blends together in fiction. reality. in the memory of the massacre. what happened. who was responsible. oblivion. repression. denial. *spectral analysis. as spectral analysis.* objects of comparison. to do justice. I don't know. I don't know. the art of making one word speak several times. *bloody cultural isn't it?*

she talked about the strata. balanced by those in power. to keep the elite at a level power could. can. accept. generations of intellectual elite. she says. I love her gestures. when she speaks. when her hands draw sharply how thin this stratum is. geopolitical crack. in the dense matter. the tunnel. to be buried alive. to get out. a single beam of light. to become this primitive urge. out. up. through. becoming one with it. recovering in it. when everything flickers. slides. the outer images penetrate far too far into the inner. to just widen and widen. hit the same spot. or an ever-softer movement. supple. swift. unpredictable. suddenly without a landscape. I envy her her landscape. yes she says. I probably seek out the places where the layers of language are not as thick. where it's a thinner membrane. I was totally in your hands. secret connection. the word she uses. *connections*. almost. the broken language. the broken history. Germany, Russia. history of the empires. the sensitivity. intelligence. the calm relationship. to genius. hypersensitivity. language's passion. hurt. whereas nobody wanted to understand. nobody wanted to bestow. reading's space. blooming spring onion. Sigurd. the song of grief. revenge. refugees streaming into Turkey. Russian special forces entering the country. burning outlines. as. as you are. in mine

a woman in a bright red dress stands in the middle of the street with a banner.
all alone. *stop the killing.* she waves the fabric between the cars. rain in the streets.
muggy air. the dark of weariness. not humor's agility. its quicksilver movements.
rising rapidly. thirty peace observers. eighteen dead. one day. in one day. during the
truce. watched the weapon penetrate steel. the airless triangle. the gas expanding. the
rotating bullet. how it pierced the decimeter-thick steel. armor plating. the armored
tank. whirling whirling. in the April night. the undead. around the heart. the torso.
the film she says over and over. the moving image. a black lacquered glittering
membrane. long silences. foghorns. fusions. *there is no repeat.* ahead is only.
language's silence and injury. taboo. vacuum. *the gesture's language. the guest's.*
which will pierce the skin. the blank look. surveillance equipment. money with
blood. systematic rape. sixty thousand. numbers. not names

strains of fire across the landscape. impossible to put out. *no bread next year.* several kilometers. Idlib province. security service. the snipers. saw gulls over the dark water. the summer night sky mirrored. bright fields. away from the city. a few minutes. nautical miles. the gravity perhaps. in the sensation. the dread. in proportion to. the white nights. the rising light. waterfowl. richly nuanced. plumage. injured words. the well. something deeper. sudden tears. you have to catch it. in the winter. the endlessly beautiful winter landscape. or something much more unstable. the movement itself. the expectation. the hope. the non-place. outlined so sharply. the image of the dead children. Hama. their throats cut. with knives. fifty of them. curled tight together on the ground. the blanket. the dried blood. the open eyes. empty. the angle between head and body. streaks of blood across the face. do you see what it is he asks. pointing to another image. I see. a boy leaping. mid-jump. floating. in mid-air. over several. many. long. lines. of white-wrapped bodies. life and death he says. such a strange picture. he says. as if he is playing

Abu Dhabi | Rub' al Khali

The sun he says when the plane takes off from Doha.

See it?

You thought it was the moon.

You say so.

It looks like the moon.

You watch the sunset over the bay. The city.

During landing.

Structures you think.

To sprint at the right moment.

Take what can be taken.

Wet snow the First of May you read.

Arise ye workers sings inside you.

Since something has to sing.

In the capitalist dictatorship.

Nine hundred thousand citizens.

The rest are laborers. For various high or low wages.

Without civil rights.

Papers.

You fall asleep. Almost.

A feeling of danger wakes you.

Take me with you you say.

No he says.

It's hot. I'll be searching for the place for a long time.

You keep swimming until you see him leave.

The tall buildings.

Oil is the answer to almost every question.

Qatar is only gas.

Everything is gas.

In the white light.

There's no light in the desert he says.

It's totally dark now. When there's no moon.

We wouldn't see anything.

We won't get to the desert you think.

Trust me he says.

No you answer.

Is it sexy you ask about the belly dancing.

I don't know he answers.

Prostitutes they say. About the women entering.

From Morocco.

The Moroccan government has instituted prostitution.

He'd already said on the plane.

All men have done it he says.

No you say.

In the dark in the wholly artificial world.

You look into his eyes.

The eyes you still can't decide the color of.

It's all empty inside you.

A yellow stripe on the horizon.

Damp heat.

Endless lines of cars on the roads.

Expensive cars.

You see a white bus going down the straight road.

Distinct in the haze.

It's painful you say.

Do they hide.

Do they hide with their friends.

How do they know who is a friend. And who an enemy.

I would die here you say.

It would kill me.

Don't spend my time for nothing he says when you refuse to speak.

Haven't you ever seen a class system before. India for example.

No you answer.

She lost the baby his friend says.

The doctors said she would have another miscarriage if she traveled.

I said so to the man.

I'd do anything for you to extend her visa.

You just have to sign the paper.

He refused.

She was forced to travel.

Across the border and back.

Had a miscarriage.

Lost the baby.

I have no memories here he says.

I don't remember when I get to Dubai how I got there.

I don't remember what I did yesterday or last week.

When people ask me how old I am I always answer twenty-four.

The age I was when I came here.

You're thinking about betrayal among the fountains and the glitter.

Ninety percent of the world is like this he says. What did you expect?

I feel like this he says and puts his hand around his throat.

You watch him stare off into space.

Don't be childish he says.

American nightmare. Not dream.

American dream without freedom he laughs.

A hysterical laughter almost capsizing into crying.

So sad and poor he says. All the Syrians who are here.

A free act. The movement of the cars on the parallel highways.

Until everyone is worn out they will allow the war to continue he says.

It will take a hundred years before it's again a country to live in.

Trust me. We'll get to the desert he says.

I don't trust you you answer.

We're already in it he says.

There's sand everywhere he laughs.

The houses are built right on it. In it. Higher and higher.

I don't listen to music any longer his friend says.

Not Arabic. Just black metal.

The old man starts to cry as he tells you.

About the day he entered Shatila.

He stops when he gets to the girl's dress. The blue stitches.

He starts over.

I could only take pictures of the horses they had shot in the head he says.

I came in a different way.

With a woman. A photographer.

We rode a motorcycle. Came to a barrier.

I knew each path in the camp like my own hand.

Each path into it.

I saw a backhoe at the far end of the road.

Watched it work.

Only later did I understand he says.

It was pushing dead bodies down into the wet cement.

I saw a pile.

Went closer.

Saw a group of people who had been tied together by their feet
and dragged behind cars.

Alive.

Their bodies had swollen.

Their clothes were torn.

The stitches.

You leave the city. You don't understand where you're heading

There's nowhere you can stop.

Because of the security cameras.

He drives you through the darkness.

You open the window.

See sand dunes along the road.

Fences to keep out the camels.

The old borders between the Emirates.

You drive onto a road that doesn't appear on the GPS.

Has no name.

He doesn't stop.

It might be a military zone his friend says.

They might be filming us right now he laughs.

You drive further. Stop at a gas station.

They get out of the car.

Stay here they say.

And go to buy coffee. Water. Chewing gum.

You come to the hills.

The ones he wanted you to drive three hours to see.

The hills of sand.

Dark silhouettes.

A valley.

You watch him disappear into it like a shadow.

It's not deep he ascends saying.

You go back to the car.

Drive through Dubai.

The extreme architecture.

Skyscrapers.

Wealth. Cars.

You watch the world's tallest building for a few seconds.

Speeding by.

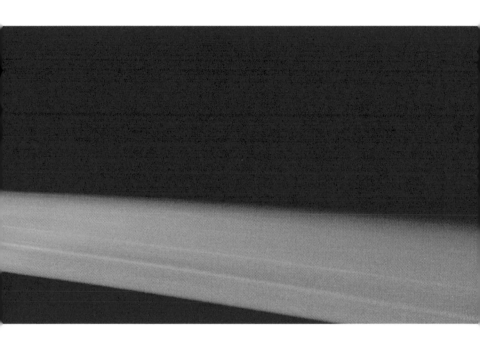

You hear his friend's laughter for the first time.

Their hushed voices.

Fall asleep to the sound.

You look at the lights in the evening.

The five-star hotel on the other side of the water.

The fountains.

You think about the confusion.

The silence.

The knocks on the door.

To be a witness you say.

To retell what you've seen when asked.

A duty says the old man. Yes. But I can't.

It's in my poems in other ways.

As metaphysics. Sufism.

You feel my emotions in your body he says.

Cries.

from **Seen Thus | the City is a Double Oblivion**

a cluster of consonants. consonant-dense words. you shook the blood. you glow on girls' eyelids. who cares about the laws of the land. he puts a hand to my back, pushes me toward the center. but I shake my head. it's good he says. but I loose myself from his grasp. in the drizzle. darkness. nouns. repetitions. handwriting. to write by hand. with the hand. every syllable. letter. let the ruin in. open to it. touch death. the loss of someone's face. you're standing on a razor. I hear the birds. it's raining. raining. rained yesterday. we smoked in the drizzle. it rained when we went out. it cooled us off. the rain. it rained as I walked through the park. it's raining now. I turned off the movie. couldn't stand watching all the precariousness. the threat. so hard to place. the scaffolding. the lack of safety. the falling body. I'm slipping I'mslipping. a brown arm. the body falling from someone's hands. acts of solidarity. one after another. gets fired. dismissed. picked up by the police. falls. early morning. autumn chill in the air. heat haze. thin veils of cloud gather and cover the sun. details she repeats. almost stammers. as if her crying could start. any second now. *details*. a lost wholeness. lost hope of wholeness. splintered country. divided. occupied. lacking connections. extensions in space. a barbarism to write after slavery. even. he says. propaganda's image. a whole world's indifference. to speak against it. be heard. details. to survive. just live. defeat. of great ideals. inner defeats the delicate movements. of the soul. through the park. the place of. arrival. departure. no. he says. a feeling through the park. to have touched. precisely that space. in the autumn night's darkness. the damp. *the first day. got away. I can't any longer. my head is.* those who could get out of the country. walking through the park I realize it's the same space. as the frost crystals. he sits on the edge of the bed. I stand in the window smoking. when did we have this discussion. self-hatred and poetry. twofold. not just poison and healing. pleasure and torment. knife and flame. *the poem and the executioner.* the handprint on the inner wall. when it is leveled. the hand comes to a standstill. in great openness. wonder

see a rainbow from the train window

and then another one

they fill the whole curve from earth to sky

or vice versa

I'm so tired

I can't walk he says

shows me the swollen veins

of his hand, wrist

a white feather floats on the breeze

between the houses

in the sun

the still-warm September sun

again

and then another

can't understand it's the same

if it is

can't understand the day or the night

or the tears

or their

absence

I hear the soughing of the big trees in the park

through the open windows

someone's playing the violin

for a long time

what a beautiful pronunciation I say

the streams

of blue, red

whirling

it rained constantly

a thick carpet of grey rain

from the grey sky

the girl in the forest I'm thinking of

for a long time

en annan sort

one hundred spices in the rice

he says while we watch

the globe rotating

on the screen

or the satellite above the globe

Madagascar

Sri Lanka

India

the ice

turn my head

see Mount Everest rising above the earth's surface

pomegranate honey

how you let the juice run, darken

sweet

like pomegranate

sour

like pomegranate

the honey

I didn't listen

heard nothing

couldn't taste the flavor

saw steam rising from the bread

all newly

baked

sensed the warmth

not the flavors

there was a story

the bullet

it takes

to justify

lovers

galán de noche. the fragrance. drifted in through the car window. a similar name in Arabic. like the perfume he says. my mother planted it in our garden. the fragrance fills the whole area. at night. city of jasmine. Damascus. a whole forest of fruit trees several thousand years old. that the president cut down. devastated. built housing on

the shifting landscape outside the bus window. red soil. the road. like the one between Damascus and Daraa he says. a volcanic eruption. a hard plateau. red dirt. at times his eyes. as if they sometimes entered zones of extreme light. he looks away

displacement. an instrument for measuring distances. by the stars. seafarers. a floating image. *life and death matter.* hands in the water. up to the wrists. the scope of the world's simultaneity. in the body. bodies. between them

maybe I'm just a bad person
we all are

De Wilde See | Léopoldville

A woman starts talking with you at the airport.

She asks which train to take.

The one that's about to come you say.

She follows you into the train car.

Looks out the window as the train slowly moves.

Over the flat green landscape in the rain.

She says she's happy to be in Europe.

Happy to be among the green fields.

It's so peaceful she says.

You ask her about the lake.

Mirror Lake.

With its many-colored reflections.

In Sichuan Province.

I've never been there she answers.

I live nearby but have never been there.

She writes down her address.

You-you she says.

Asking you to read her name aloud.

My relatives will be at Platform One in a few hours she says.

You don't have to wait.

He takes your suitcase.

Write me she says.

You sensed walls in the dream.

The dream you woke from.

You open the window.

One of the small windows facing the quiet street.

The tram had stopped shaking the house.

It was hot.

He slept.

You read about the trade agreement between China and the Netherlands.

You walk along the canal.

See how it branches.

The delta.

The enormous harbor.

Cranes.

The square and the alleys are full of living statues.

A woman melts into the relief at the cathedral.

Green-painted like the oxidized copper.

She gets up.

When someone puts money into the bowl at her feet.

Blinks.

Curtseys.

You walk through Chinatown.

A single long straight street.

He leads you into another.

I want you to see it he says.

Women sit at the windows.

The doors.

Of glass.

Opened halfway.

You watch the men in the street.

Their faces.

The blend of excitement and shame.

A ridiculous amused expression.

You watch a man press his face against the glass.

Stare.

With hate.

The woman tries to move out of his sight.

Tempts him.

To move.

He keeps on.

Presses his face against the glass at the height of her sex.

Pulls his face away.

Backs up a few steps.

Looks at her.

Forces his face against the glass again.

A family stands by an open door.

You see their worn clothes.

A heavily pregnant woman stands in the doorway a half step above.

While a man converses with the family in the street.

You see a note about renting rooms on the house wall.

You write You-you. Get no reply.

The Flemish couple explains bells.

The chiming for four hours.

Tell you about the name.

The thrown hand. Ant werp.

In remembrance of someone who cut off his hand after slaughtering many people.

For some god or ruler.

And stopped.

By cutting his own hand off.

And now stands erected as a statue in the square.

If it's collective memory.

Or collective amnesia.

You wonder.

Ten million.

Hands. Mutilations.

In the colonies.

You look at the façade of the newly built historical museum.

A small silver hand in each rust-red stone.

Waar.

No. It doesn't mean war answers the Flemish man.

About the word engraved on the floor.

Not war.

Truth.

You don't go into the zoo.

You go and look in the shop windows.

The long lines of diamond shops at the station.

It's a mafia says his friend.

The ones who cut them.

The blood diamonds.

From Sierra Leone.

Coltan. Tantalum.

The minerals in all smartphones. Laptops.

A sound.

As if each object suddenly screamed out its price.

In child labor. Worn-down human bodies.

You walk together through the tunnel.

More than five hundred meters long.

Thirty-one meters under the river's surface.

You get up in the night.

Wake up when you hear him walking over the sloping floor.

Gravity is good you say in the café.

When he lets his hand hang down to release the tension. The pain.

Do you still remember it he answers as you enter.

When you say he has said it before.

A long time ago.

You disturb the Sufis.

The sound of your heels clacking over the narrow metal walkway.

You make so much noise.

Don't disturb the Sufis.

You hear him sit down and sigh heavily.

With each breath.

You listen to the sighs.

Hear the music coming from the speakers.

You walk together to the tram.

See the rails in the cobblestones.

The train starts to roll.
In the other direction.

You board the plane.
It fills up with men in suits.
Locked in their headphones.
Sleeping. Dozing.
Eyes shut.

The meteor you think.
Thou shall not thou me.

Snow Revolution

felt the trauma.   the violence without anesthesia the pain

what you whisper in the night. to whom   *what is this. the cold. I'm really*

contained in their night   or the lack of

nomadic tenderness. nomadic

repelling   something volatile and flammable

the reversals   to open oneself up to

as if the violence had penetrated. or advanced into   the body. the respiratory tract

to breathe inside the vortex. the snow

the flame. the human difference

mortality   the outlines of the lungs

spectacular

a quality. of suppression. gone too deep. *normal. I want it to*

be normal. like Ukraine. responses. standpoints. spontaneous protests. actions

looked at them. at the snow fallen over the park. the trees. darkness and light

streetlamps. *so many pictures*

listened

to the language. what I understood

carried the phone through the night

away from emotion

she started crying. he embraced her. the woman who shaved her head. got through the blockade. into Homs. I wish I'd died there she says. we hoped for democracy. that it would come to us. the democracies in the West. we broke through. the wall of fear. they've put a price on her head he says. I'm against weapons she says. insists. it's the people who started and organized the revolution who should build the country she says. not the opposition abroad. who haven't lived that experience. the challenge now. is to keep retaliations from erupting. he has opened the borders. the people have begun to turn to them. out of disappointment. she refuses to read poems. in front of an audience. speaks in short sentences that are simultaneously interpreted. with big gaps. errors. of the interpreter. more and more helplessly caught in the moment. the Syrian people. she says. their poem. a list of names. lines of poetry. the young woman cries while showing the film. talking about the dead photographer. who was shot while getting into the car. that was to take him to the airport. away from Homs. we want to think he chose to stay with us she says. he taught the young journalists how to film. the brave journalists. a man with a camera runs in the film across a road monitored by snipers. the camera wheels. captures power lines. the sky. a huge explosion. is heard. then his funeral. in darkness. red light. her voice breaks as she cries. I didn't want it to come to this she says. enters the stage again. to say. you wanted us to feel. to be those who express and incarnate the suffering. and then your experts would talk. you didn't even ask. us. I regret she later says. I didn't allow him to film my face. you're the first person I've ever told this. I wish my face were in his films now

in time   *out of time*

belong to the conjugation. belong to

twelve twelve twelve twelve

white writing

scent-streaks

still existing? in human hands? thoughts? actions?

prime time

the other's other

how much. if there's a difference of degrees

the revolution's opposite

the situation in China. a construction of the other

brutalized consciousness

a brutalizing that has gone on for centuries

the conqueror's desire for peace. collection. of objects. words. on the objects. articles. when communities are crushed. the living deprived of the potential of speech

more at ease in a big area

the face. the ghost landscape

the white place. the empty space

there is no accident

no beginning no end

       this is the first time I'm using glass as a medium

what justifies one's speech, words?

        what's the background? the backing? the plunge?

the vertigo gripped me. for the second time. or seventh. thirtieth. not deep enough.
not words enough. in the depths. nor actions. I don't know. the house is burning.
a fire in the night. Mariaberget. the carbon heating. the stove. they go home. or stay.
I don't know. it's burning in

        to submit to something. the expectation

I lost contact with my first painting on glass and I've started another one

sisters of mercy. Menon. the community

        happiness is only subversive when it's shared

    you smell like Berlin

        in the middle of the night. the politics. the avoidance

        no words I say. sad. I say

     the wall of fear

unable to carry the face. the body

the division of Syria and Lebanon

Lebanon was the mountain. the coast. the center. the opening to the sea. how

France could divide it   into four countries

the tree line. if it's there the non-control begins

a completely free fall

an opened

sacred circle. the blown-over

trees. autumn storm. roots. windthrow

the capacity to imagine. catch fire

if France apologized to Algeria. the

strong to the weak. 45,000 killed. in one day. then it would change

things

the mentality

I leaned my cheek against the wall

a cloud of freckles. tangled spheres. hard to say in which face
                              now it's breaking apart
nothing I say. I feel nothing

      we wrote about Damascus in the nick of time before its destruction he says
the deep Orient he says. deep city. everything is more real. the poverty. the richness
Cairo is only one thousand years old
                              Aleppo is totally destroyed. with fire

before the revolution. he smiles. when I say we'll remember this time. when sixty percent
of people lived alone in their apartments as those in Petersburg remember the kom-
munalka. the kommunalka experience

      he's a small poet he said Adonis answered about F. and refused to sign the
petition for his release. if I. also a small poet. were in jail. would you do it for me?
he asked. standing there with the unsigned paper. then they parted. never saw each
other again

                    explosion of despair

                    they suddenly rose and held each other. she'd received a
phone call. she cried softly. into his shoulder
                              such thin bodies. in their clothes. jeans

this other voice. because the foundation will never be sealed. because the place where it
could appear cannot be found. can only be invoked. only exist if invoked

    life is full of paradoxes. people are

      breathe he said   the warning labels

you're so sensitive

I've heard it before. from other people

what's this day called?

cross or birth?

                                                     disaster

                                      Columbus hotel

          and if sleep won't come

crystallize. the condition

                              the body woke up. in the middle of the night

              almost full moon

                        refusing time

              white photographs

black letters

                              give back our sun

                  to hand each other

                        shelterless language

Bárðarbunga

A blue sulfur fog from the eruption lies over the city.

A thin haze.

You smell sulfur even in the shower.

See low wooden houses. Corrugated metal.

A small plane flies in for a landing.

It rains.

You get soaking wet.

Eat noodle soup.

The meat tastes different. Denser.

You listen to Chinese being spoken as the rain pours down outside.

You walk out into it.

Ask about the boat.

We'll get back to you the woman answers.

You see the whale meat's blood-red color in the display case.

Try to drink coffee outside in the harbor and smoke

the only cigarette left in your pocket.

The rain whips in from the sea.

You swim in a large outdoor swimming pool.

A long time.

As if through the volcano.
The lava streams.

Epilepsy. Visions.
A blue juice.

A woman starts talking to you in the dressing room.
Says she recognizes you. Has seen you often.
It's my first time you say.

You see a rainbow across the sky.
A film about the ocean you say.
How the island lies in the ocean.
Deep in our memory.

You meet a woman from Uruguay.
With grandparents from Poland and Hungary.
Now living in Australia.
Outside the apartment she rents she tells you
garbage piles up.
One morning she saw a woman up to her waist in the mountain of trash.

Using a tool to scoop something edible out of it.

A man and a woman from Montreal next to you stiffen.

Really?

Wealth has returned hasn't it they say.

Could they have done something better you ask a woman.

2008.

Something more radical she answers.

You walk to the flea market in a large shed.

See hand-knit sweaters. Bracelets of lava stones.

The books in the river.

Totally tinged blue from the ink.

You remember.

The devastated city.

The stage's memory she says.

The ghost in Hamlet.

How to interpret it for the deaf.

Only later you imagine confusing the sounds.

A theater for the dead.

An analogy between gift loss and spectacle she says.

When you give what is most precious to you.

You become nothing.

You see the glass greenhouses. Warmed with steam.

How they glow in the dark landscape.

The biggest desert in Europe he says.

Lava fields.

Two thousand or twenty thousand big or small earthquakes per week.

Continental plates.

They slide apart at two centimeters per year he says.

As you pass over the crevice between the Eurasian

and the American.

In other places they converge he says.

At the Himalayas for example.

The longest period without sun since records began he says.

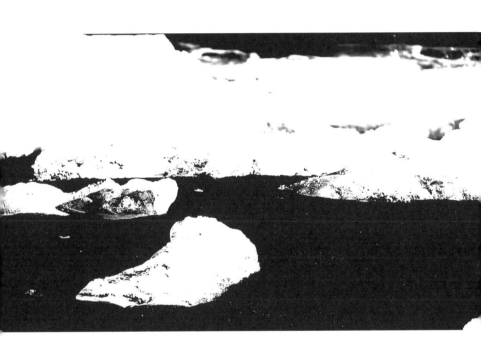

But you don't hear in which decade or century.

You wait a long time for the geyser to jet.

At last it does.

Jets.

In the downpour.

You take a step back when it happens.

See the bubble expanding seconds prior.

Smell the sulfur.

The waterfall.

Cascades.

The huge mist of water droplets.

The similarities between Iceland and Japan you're thinking of.

If similarities exist.

Not tonight either will the ship depart for the northern lights.

A woman calls to say.

The hottest place on earth he says.

Under the glaciers.

Exploding lava when the volcano erupts.

And the melting glacier flows down into the crater.

Or the lava that flowed into the lake and was cooled down.

Was so hot it became so light it could float on water.

A new continent she said.

A way of living.

Not a country.

Or a city.

The bottom of a deep fjord.

The uplift is still ongoing.

You see a brimstone butterfly at Eyjafjallajökull.

The whole summer of 2010 I drove through black clouds he says.

Two lava streams. One on each side of the village.

Do the Japanese care about the French Revolution you think.

When he tells you it's said that the big eruption of 1780

triggered the Revolution.

The famine it caused in Europe.

Long years of black clouds covering half the continent.

You arrive at a black lava beach full of huge ice blocks.

Nowhere.
To Antarctica you come.
If you go straight south he says.

A Japanese woman falls asleep on the bus. Then another.
They look like people in the subway in Tokyo.
Their heavy sleep.

Hong Kong she says they come from when you finally ask.

You don't want to be in the rain a minute longer.
But change your mind when you enter the room.
Run toward the boat.
Just before it casts off into the dark.
Reykjavik disappears.
The rain ceases.
The cold intensifies.

But you notice it only later. When the cold has pervaded your body.

Strangely happy.

You listen to the captain as he reads in his Icelandic accent

blush upon the cheek of night

posthumous, unearthly light

You circle.

Stop still.

Nothing happens.

People go below deck.

Fall asleep at the table.

You climb up again.

The northern lights the captain says coming next to you.

Points.

Can you see it?

A white cloud. Barely.

Maybe.

I'm used to it he says.

That's why.

I see the activity.

How many hours of time difference you think.

How hours are counted.

From a place that's still young.

Geologically speaking.

Short minutes of joy are so rare now he writes.

Russia is reaching hell in full rage.

A fontanelle you think.

Where the world opens. Upward. On the globe.

Rotating continuously. In its gravity.

Eat it with your mouth closed the host says.

About the rotten shark.

Let your tongue taste it.

And let the taste rise into your forehead.

Chug the liquor.

Down the whole glass.

Snow

to keep standing in the attempt. the strata giving way. the negative. the lighting. longer. heavier. darker. burial in red light. to forget the name and remember only the word. nuclear fission. rejection. secretion. fortified borders. the rearmament. if the nerve gas falls into rebel hands. the announcement. the reaction. a cord of pain along the abdomen's skin. his hand movements when he describes how they loaded a car full of rockets that didn't explode on impact. how with the help of remote control they drove the car right into the government army camp. images of snow. a grill in snow with skewers of snow. a collection of snow figures to mourn the dead. the dead body. in snow. the mourners. in snow. the ground covered. while the refugee camps fill with freezing people. the tents groan under the snow. Esperanza. the boat. in the hell of hope. turbulence. the book in the river. in the aftermath. 23.15. oceanic time. capital of pain. the strait. the movements. nicht. nacht. hush. echoland. the rations. the scales. what does it mean to give and take he asks. and answers himself: sleep. and repeats the question throughout the night. what does it mean to give and take. he hears the dying man through his sleep. his last words. what does it mean to give and take

wake up and see faces. T's, J's. wake up and look out into the winter night.
snow over the fields. the forest. to pass through the pain and know it

if he screams brother. or his name. in the film. is laid bare. listener she says. street sweeper. ten days later the attack began. my legs shook. my body. we laughed at all the jokes about solutions. bombs fell the whole night. ceasefire. as it breaks through. in the call signals. the conversations. a closed door. an open face. straight stroke. the city between the bridges. not a bridge. igniting rapidly. then sleep. long. Winter Road. the Road of the Northern Lights. echo sounder. or hunger's cessation. white roofs. whirling snow. language's enigma. no turning back. who says that. who lit this flame in us. what is the flame. the human difference. the difference. human actions. every night. each night. I'll lie awake asking myself this question. zones of clarity. moments. my bare hands. wrists. some points of contact. some likeness. it woke me. fell asleep again. inner figure. blaze. conscience. tenderness. living or dead eyes. at some point when we're talking. I see his eyes become alive. a noise he utters. physically. from deep within his body. as the eyes deepen. feel it in the movement between us. opening up. feel the fear. the nausea. a cold wind. methods. for torturing female prisoners. books get burned in order to write new ones. the journey is dissolving. the boat on the river. the gaze out into the white light. what kind of creeping madness was it that won our city over? I hear a voice saying on the radio. he breathes as if he has fallen asleep. I look at him. walk across the bridge. save the book. do you want to smoke he asks oblique light. oblique slant of light. wet snow

reach to touch L's outstretched fingertips across the table

you are my emerald he says

you mine

third body. the anatomy of the relation. to erase. say his name. forget. to release. what the morning did not contain. or hadn't enclosed within. what vanity I laughed. no it's not vanity he said and slugged me on the arm. not vanity. to master eleven languages. to walk in the dark. with both hands. tracing. along the scar. *treason. scar.* its opposite. a waving motion over the letters. in the letters. I fell asleep for a micro-second. screamed he's here

he's not here. I did not betray him. I was freezing the whole time. a pain in the body. to enter the skin. a moment. a few days. a rotation. of equilibriums. canceled out. sought after. independent and interdependent. money flows. the abrupt emergency brake. riots in Europe. poverty. evictions. demonstrations. police brutality. the prohibition on photography. on recording. arrests of those who do. bruises on the boy's hands. legs. the woman leaned against a man I couldn't see. her half-closed eyes. slow speech. something running down her face. in the midst. a distance. a worn jacket. maybe unsettled still. une communauté. a whirlwind. internal. wholly internal. the first snow. the white roofs. a woman leans her head against the handrail on the bus. as if completely overpowered by fatigue. while her two children. one in a stroller. the other beside her. are completely still

Cape Point

You see the face of a house sharply sketched.

Near the harbor.

On the street you turn into.

A light over the façade.

Like a flash.

Of a photograph that's taken.

You start crossing the street.

Toward the other sidewalk.

But only make it halfway.

Two men come rushing toward you. Shouting.

Quickly search your body. Take the phone from your back pocket.

Lift the camera from your shoulder.

Drop the charger.

Run off.

You pick it up.

See a man sitting in a car.

You beat the cord hard against a streetlamp.

Walk up the stairs.

See the sun over the Indian Ocean.

The construction on the left hill.

An outermost point.

Loud noise from the harbor.

Cars.

Or if it's the sound of the ocean.

All night.

The scene in your head.

The speed. The fear.

Every theft is a theft of love.

A beach.

The Indian Ocean.

A harbor facing Goa.

The struggle with the Arabs. The Portuguese. Englishmen.

Mandela's name.

The sixty-seven years he served his country.

If only you could see a single white person

gathering shopping carts in the parking lot.

Work.

The sound of construction.

Sirens.

You don't like the heat. Not the light.

Haze over the ocean. The body. Its vulnerability. The refusal inside.

A chasm. The steepness.

The brown people she says.

Take public transportation.

People swerve out of the way when they go by she says and laughs.

The first day.

An outermost point.

Light falls over it.

The horn. The eastern and the western side.

You always panic he says.

No.

Not always.

Panicking you answer.

The haze over the ocean has let up.

Big cargo ships. A railway.

Rusty freight cars.

The sun sets earlier.

It gets chilly quick.

A blue light from the ocean. A bay.

You hear car doors closing. A dog barking.

My words are like fire.

Morning over the Indian Ocean.

Why me.

The wind is blowing. Hard.

Sugar something.

Dawn arrives.

You slept in his deep sleep.

The wind is strong.

Some cargo ships move across the sea.

Why do you stress yourself.

The skin. The scent.

Afternoon. Already.

Sugar something.

Or the time that comes after a long morning.

You lay down on the couch.

Watched the dawn.

Brewed coffee. Gave him some.

The ribs.

As if broken.

The injury reopened.

How can you fuck all the time he says.

Gets up. Grabs his clothes.

Reaches for your hip.

You fuck with my head.

They understand you better than me you say.

You call them.

Whiteness is not a language.

You see a Black man on a fire escape.

Domestic workers. Mixed-race. Lack of belonging he says.

Sugar something.

You know what I mean.

The sugar road. Not just that of the diamonds.

A foghorn sounds in the dark morning.

There were poor people before you were born.

And there will be poor people after you've died.

The lit-up freight boats anchored. The outermost point. Stanley Street.

His scent on your skin.

The shock when you walk into the room and see him in his undershirt.

They were paid in wine he says. Alcohol. Everyone is an alcoholic.

You took a taxi while darkness still lay over the city.

Sat at the bus station and talked.

The others waiting there finally stopped staring.

Mixed they said when you entered the restaurant.

He didn't hear it.

Everything you later said arose from your shame about the system.

Whose laws were written at a university he pointed out when you rode by.

They didn't even speak to me.

You fell asleep. Woke up.

In the bus through the landscape.

Saw it change. The greenness.

Rainforest. Mountains.

Like in Nigeria he says.

Plains. Mountains.

Grazing sheep.

In the sunlight they look like lions.

When the police stop the bus and ask him for his ID.

He looks away. Delays answering.

We'll be back they say and start at the back of the bus.

They will never ask you.

He almost spits out.

Because you're white.

But they do.

Just as aggressively.

Thanks for telling me you say.

When they say they're doing it for your own good.

We have to change that narrative he says to

a man across the aisle.

That all of us from Nigeria steal.

There are two hundred million of us.

Most are hardworking.

You long to rest your head against his shoulder.

But don't.

If you put a *with* there it becomes something else.

The broken rib.

Fuck with.

Your question makes him so furious he falls silent.

Racial injustice. Not economic injustice.

A house is burning near Cape Town.

The fire department doesn't come.

They have to put out the fire themselves he says.

If not then the whole area will burn down.

White supremacists.

Fog over the city.

Still dark. Cold. Skyscrapers. Long Street.

Fields of distrust. Drugs. Hookers.

You doze off. Against the window.

Somehow. Did I sleep well.

How are you.

Too chaotic.

Three men sit and speak in Afrikaans at the table. On the balcony.

You see the fog.

The mountain.

The street below.

Fire that glows. Burns.

The men watch you as you go in and out.

Morning says the man with a patch on his eye when they get up.

Whale Street.

All signs in Afrikaans.

Why do you call out the numbers in Afrikaans the woman in line said when
no one reacted at number ninety.

I don't understand she said.

The woman at the counter looked at you to back her up.

What did you do with that gaze.

Don't know.

I-don't-know.

He laughs at you.

Names you.

They all moved here when apartheid was dismantled he says.

Brought all their riches with them.

Joburg where the government is located. ANC.

They didn't want to be close.

Morning.

A dry cleaner's on the other side of the street is already open.

The moment you say.

You stroke the sole of his foot.

Leafing through the book.

Sorry for disturbing you.

Come to Nigeria.

A trail that forks.

A trail that opens.

To be swallowed by the road.

A Yoruba belief.

Now you have to take a shower again.

No. I like your smell.

Interesting he replies.

You see the opening in the harbor toward Robben Island.

When you come out of the museum fog is covering the whole area.

The South Pole is closest in kilometers a sign says.

You long for his smell.

You turn around.

But your stomachache comes back along the way.

If it's the outermost point.

That apartheid was adopted in 1948.

How could it be moved.

Did they move here.

Anne Frank's story is displayed at the museum.

Which has no visitors except for you.

The tickets to the ferry are sold out.

You get back in line.

But change your mind when you hear an American exchange

his reservation for a ticket.

Black tourism. Dark.

You don't remember what it's called.

His laughter. That you wanted to live inside. You got to live inside.

Aimed at you.

Bob Marley. He was the best.

Says a man in Green Market Square.

No man no cry.

Why have none of us women in the whole world written that song you wonder.

You're my first customer she says.

I'll give it to you for three hundred.

You meet him on the street.

Suddenly he's walking down Long Street.

In his black jacket.

He just stops.

Stands still. Says nothing.

Reproaching. Reproach. Worry.

They said you took a map and went out.

You asked them?

Do you know how long you've been gone he says.

Five hours.

You think it's seven.

You don't say it.

Stroke his arm.

Take his hand.

His little finger with yours.

I'm going to exchange some money he says.

They told me there's a black market exchange at a hair salon across from a hotel.

Go to Western Union the man says when you've entered the inner room.

It's because I'm from Nigeria he says when you walk out.

Or because you're with a white woman you say.

He laughs.

Conformists he says. Of his generation.

I'm not stupid.

I hear you.

No. You're not stupid.

Spices and silk she says.

Diamonds. Gold. She doesn't say.

I throw you.

At the Cape of Good Hope.

The Cape of Storms.

It couldn't be named.

No hot water?

You know there is.

Indigenous forest.

The Dutch cut down the trees in 1652.

Planted Italian pines.

So that the sand wouldn't erode she says.

Seal colonies in the Atlantic.

Near where the two oceans meet.

Big waves.

Hout Bay.

False Bay.

Long Beach.

Quicksand.

Holland needed a garden.

On the way to India she says.

So the sailors wouldn't get scurvy.

Cape Point.

Cape of Storms.

The Atlantic.

The cliff face.

I throw you.

The lighthouse.

Where two oceans meet.

The Indian Ocean and the Atlantic.

One warm. One cold.

Some currents. But otherwise nothing dramatic she says.

Far out in the ocean you see four whales.

Round rings in the water.

The place of the winds.

The windiest place in South Africa.

A troop of baboons cross the road.

The ones that have learned to feed from the sea.

It's good for us.

What do you need rain for?

Drought.

Wild almond.

They were planted between the colonizers and the locals she says.

Like a border.

The fruit is poisonous.

It looks like an octopus. I think. She says.

In 1902 Cecil Rhodes donated

all the land for the botanical garden.

Yes she says. He was a racist. I will not lie to you.

How to do things with words you think.

When you pass a location far away from the wealthy white houses.

And she's talking about the satellite disks.

And then you see them.

And hardly anything else.

Not the poverty.

Not the density.

You only have to pay three hundred rand she says.

A one-time payment. For life.

But it only transmits a few channels.

My mother died a month ago she suddenly says.

It was my first impulse.

To come here to the botanical garden.

We were always here when I was a child.

The adults sat on the grass.

We ran all the way up into the mountains.

He took plants and trees from all corners of the world with him.

And planted them here she says.

To see which ones would root and grow.

The garden of the colonizers.

Donated terrain.

Give back the land.

The sentence he erased.

The passage.

Why are you undressing me and not yourself?

I'm going to take a walk.
Alone?
No you can join me.

He beats against the wallpaper with the naked female body parts.
White.
Saying stop looking at me.
He doesn't get up immediately.
Stroking your hips.

What are you thinking about he asks again at the airport.
About you you answer.
Go back to Istanbul he says.
Think of Istanbul.
She should stay inside until things calm down.
Then she can go.

Feminists with children are now welcome on board.

You thought you heard her saying.

You lay your head against his shoulder on the plane.

You look sexy he says in the morning.

Who are you talking to you ask.

You.

What do you want he asks.

What makes you happy.

You could answer fucking.

But don't.

When you fuck me.

Small things you answer.

Sacrifices then.

That you came here. All this long way.

You see the whorls of his ears. At the restaurant.

As if you hadn't seen them before.

From Zimbabwe the woman answers when he goes out to talk on his phone.

Papa is your husband she asks.

No a friend.

How many kids do you have.

Two.

Me too.

Daughters.

You eat with your hands.

Don't have a choice.

Watch him lick his hands.

Don't understand how the fufu can stay so clean on his plate.

Cassava he says.

You see a man pounding with a wooden pole behind the counter.

Is it a long process.

Yes.

What he says when you come in after smoking out on the street.

Why do they steal he says.

I would also steal you say if I were in this country.

This fucked up continent he says.

The tip of this fucked-up continent.

Where do you come from.

Are you talking to me boss the driver asks and turns around.

Zim boss.

Do you know any Nigerian restaurants.

Yes.

The taxi is stopped by the police.

He was drunk says the driver when he comes back.

The police told me to put something on the seat he says and sits behind the wheel.

It's like in Nigeria he says.

It's like everywhere he responds.

You are really adventurous he says at the restaurant.

What a strange street.

You looked down at the waves for a long time.

Blue. Massive.

How they were beating against the nearly vertical cliff face.

It's the end of the world he says about Nice.

Did I bring my inhaler with me he asks on the street.

You can't understand.

Everything she said. The guide. About the country.

What machinery you think.

For occupying and plundering.

Keeping the wealth.

Considering the country theirs.

How they succeeded.

Three break-ins this morning she says.

Despite the armed guards.

The last shall be the first.

Mandela's Gold in the garden.

Ten years she says it took to breed it.

He shows you music videos all evening.

From Lagos. Abuja.

That Mandela shit doesn't interest me.

It was better under the dictatorship than under democracy.

Everything is corrupt.

It's not democracy it's capitalism.

And what do you think of capitalism.

You see the cargo ships.

His white undershirt over the shower door.

Why are you breathing like this. Uneven.

I left her in the labyrinth you think.
At the white lighthouse on Cape Point.
How could I leave her in the labyrinth.

He closes the door to talk undisturbed.
Desire is always a question.
It darkens over the sea.
The ships are lit up.
The lanterns.
What a strange street.
He laughs again at the spot where you were robbed.
I can vanish you say.
I'm good at vanishing.
I'll find you in a hole he says.

I'm scared you say and go in to him.
I'll join you he says.
Like a seven-year-old child he laughs.

And lays down next to you.

You weave your feet with his.

Hear his breathing.

I'm happy if you are.

You hear his phone receive its messages.

When he has fallen asleep.

Again and again.

Somewhere out there.

The two oceans meet.

Between the two cities.

Do you call this blond he says holding a strand.

White you reply.

The sun rises over the ocean.

The cargo ships move almost magnetically toward the opening.

A line.

Glinting in the light.

You listen to the seagulls.

The sun warms you.

Through the window.

It's blowing hard.

Hungry. Angry.
You never hear the difference.

It's a man's world. He plays the song. In many versions.
Why do white people do this.
It's really misogynistic.
James Brown. 1966 he says. I was a dream then.

An apartheid weapon he says. Pointing at the baton hanging on the door.
They used to beat black people with it.

The rain reaches Port Elizabeth.
Big raindrops.
A family of dreamers.
The days end. The hours pass.
Darkness falls.
To survive the night. In the wind.
The wind picks up.
From the infinite no conclusions can be drawn.

Or the impossible.

The infinite or the impossible you try to remember.

The sun rises behind the tall houses.

Children climb the hill in their school uniforms.

A smell like brown coal enters the room.

Traffic at the harbor.

A long freight train.

Fog over the sea.

The clouds in veils and whorls.

The world washed clean of its massacres.

Not washed.

At all.

All its massacres.

From each side of the globe.

The map and the history.

The lighthouse.

Green fields.

She falls asleep next to you on the bus.

Almost everyone falls asleep.

Her head drops. Nodding. Bobbing.

She straightens up.

Then her head drops again.

Sleep and vigil.

Bird-of-paradise.

Bird of paradise flower.

The colonizer's sublime landscape.

Love they say.

Writes Coetzee.

For the country.

But the problem with mountains trees and plants is that they do not respond.

No one knows if the love is returned.

A white statue. Gleaming. The descended body. The passion.

You dream when you fall asleep for a few minutes next to him.

Waking. Dozing off.

Then fall into a deep sleep.

Did it mean danger. Rest.

You don't know any longer.

The danger has already passed.

Early morning. Silent.

He gets furious at the restaurant.

The spear he says when he sees it on the wall.

Africa he sneers. White supremacists. White privilege.

To be or not to be.

A white lover.

The road that once was a river.

And turned into a road.

And therefore always unstable.

Where they wanted to stay unborn. Yearned to return.

If they were born.

To the unborn world.

Until he saw his mother's face and didn't want to see it in sorrow.

You cannot have boots all the time he says and points

at his flip-flops.

As if you were going to stay a long time.

The white stone walls.

The bird in the morning.

The people going out for the day.

Said good morning.

The stairs where you were smoking.

The narrow ledge you sat on.

Give back the land.

To erase the passage.

Reconcile with his parents.

Their dreams.

Not with those coming after.

Let me clean this place he says and sweeps.

Spraying. Shuffling around.

The sun is already setting.

Just now there was such a beautiful afternoon light.

It still gleams over the ocean.

A boat with a red hull lies at anchor in the light.

Still.

Why are you doing this to me he says.

Why are you doing this to me you say.

You curl up against him.

I'm bad at departures.

If sleep.

Signals danger.

What a beautiful evening you say when you see the full moon outside.

My dad says that white people always talk about the beautiful days.

The beautiful weather.

For us it's just day. As it always is.

I pushed you on the side you say.

The man who walks by you in the morning says beautiful morning.

Better weather than yesterday.

Are you freaking out.

You saw a crown. A skull. A crown.

Fell asleep next to him.

Dressed.

Woke up and took off your clothes.

The bed is smaller he said in the morning.

Spicy he said about the food.

Why are you burnt he says about your face.

You are spreading your words again you say.

Stroking him over the hip. The chest.

I love your smell.

I know you do.

He lays down on his back.

But this is ejaculation.

I'm so tired.

My father warned me.

That it would stress me to be here.

Cancel your ticket and stay here. How long is your visa?

Words. Words.

Only the first half came to you.

To give what you do not have.

In the backyard.

Or the courtyard.

Your beauty always overwhelms me.

The white stone walls. The moon. Behind thin clouds.

Not quite full yet.

A man washes his car. Or someone else's car in the morning.

You see him when you go out to smoke.

Do you have three hundred rand he asks.

You walk out.

See something that could be an African raven.

I was mugged by a stereotype. Then.

He laughs.

You wake up and go down and turn on the electric water boiler.

Make coffee.

When the world or the globe spins.

The descended body. All white. Blazing.

The quiet night.

He will win you say.

The world is like that.

Now. Only a small fraction who want to own everything.

Distribute the leftovers to those willing to support them.

They've probably learned from each other.

The wall.

To build yet another one.

The roar.

Build it build it.

How that roar sounded in Europe. Just now.

Different. Silent.

It was built.

You ate some grains of rice.

I'm too sad to eat.

Rode over the plain.

Autumn light.

Bare trees.

Warmth.

Thirty-six percent unemployment in Eastern Cape.

Twenty-five percent in Cape Town.

Fifty percent in Nigeria.

All politicians are so corrupt the taxi driver says.

Plays Michael Jackson for you.

In two days you will smile again he says.

Hope is what we have isn't it?

Dawn over the Indian Ocean.

The pink clouds. How they change.

The more the sun rises.

Tiny birds land on the cactus.

Safe trip.

A foghorn is heard. Again.

The cargo ships in the haze.

Blue-white haze around the hulls.

Schoolchildren climb the hill again.

The city wakes.

Cars. Honking.

The brutal Atlantic trade.

Sirens.

The delicate birds are visible in the daylight.

With long tail feathers. A yellow feather among them.

The sun's rays in the grass outside the window.

I'm waiting he says on the stairs.

For the question you never ask.

Pulls on the waistband of your jeans.

The country below.

The green fields.

That which is glinting like silver on the ground.

If it's small rivers weaving between the green fields.

Or roads.

How the rays fall. Near the South Pole.

A lake. Peaks. Table Mountain.

Winter light over South Africa.

All Europeans look the same to me.

The low sun. In the afternoon.

Everything so slow.

The famished road.

To give what you do not have.

The long gaps in breath.

To someone.

When it begins again.

Who doesn't want it.

The breathing.

Like after a drowning.

Breathe you said.

Flying.

Falling as flying.

You went out to smoke.

You just close your eyes and open them and I'll be there.

You pant. But walk over it.

The border.

Dreamlike.

The sleep.

Deep. Gentle.

A night flight over the continent.

When you see his face. The distinct profile.

What is the relationship between South Africa and Dubai you wonder.

At Dubai's airport.

Diamonds probably.

The sun rises.

Thirty-seven degrees outside.

Cagliari. Tunis. Carthage.

The plane turns over the continent again.

The eastern side. Northern.

Was my freedom not given to me then in order to build the world of the You?

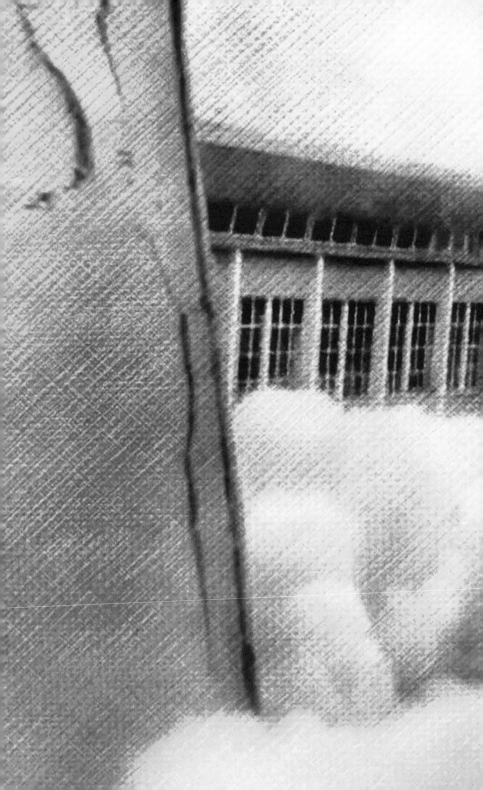

"Desire is always a question": Translating Marie Silkeberg's Poetry
Kelsi Vanada

Marie Silkeberg and I have worked together since 2015. We met when she was a visiting writer in the International Writing Program (IWP) in Iowa City, Iowa, while I was getting my MFA in Poetry at the Iowa Writers' Workshop. Using my partial knowledge of Danish (thanks to my heritage and my undergraduate study abroad), and with input from Marie, I translated a few of her poems into English for the IWP's Translation Workshop, taught by Nataša Ďurovičová. Those poems won *Asymptote's* "Close Approximations" contest the following year. In working together, We found that although her poems and mine are distinct in content, we have a kindred focus on sound, and on the positioning of the eye and the description of the visual. Many of the poems in *Damascus, Atlantis* prioritize a hyper-focus on description, the perceived world stripped of metaphor. While they can never be speakerless, these are not the poems of a lyric I.

Damascus, Atlantis includes poems from Marie's 2017 book *Atlantis*, and poems of hers from the 2014 *Till Damaskus*, written with Ghayath Almadhoun. She sees the two books as intimately linked – as different formal explorations of the same themes. Both are driven by the question of belonging. Belonging as it is (further) complicated by displacement, violence, war, and difference. The speaker(s) of, and the figures in, these poems are unnamed, often unidentified, and constantly moving. They move through each region of Europe, to the Middle East, East Asia, South Africa, and the Midwestern United States. The poems we chose for this Selected Poems are representative of both of Silkeberg's most recent books of poems, and with their visual focus it was fitting that stills from her poem films be included. All together, they create the new collage that is *Damascus, Atlantis*.

Silkeberg's poems in *Till Damaskus* are primarily comprised of blocks of text inspired by Russian painter Kazimir Malevich's 1915 *Black Square*. This iconic painting signified a pivotal shift toward non-representational art, known as "the zero point of painting."[1] Marie's poems are built of fragments, and many of the phrases seem to either extend the thought of the previous phrase or bleed into the following phrase. No punctuation is used except for periods, creating a tense pacing. In Swedish, articles attach to the ends of nouns, so I cut some of the articles in the translation to capture the immediacy of the Swedish phrases, as well as their sound, which Marie describes as "swirling." For her, the sound of these poems enacts "the vertigo, the instability of being a person in a place." *Atlantis* carries out not only the themes of *Till Damaskus*, but many of its poetic modes, especially in regard to the aforementioned positioning of the eye, leading to the aggregate, anaphoric listing quality of the observations recorded in both books.

Formally, it is distinct from *Till Damaskus*, employing brief sentences or phrases in short lines, written in what Marie calls a "stripped 'zero' language." Each word carries weight. To translate this collection into English, Marie and I spent many long sessions together (many of them on the island of Visby in 2018 during a joint residency at the Baltic Centre for Writers and Translators, for which I'm grateful). I provided multiple ways of phrasing words or lines in English for us to choose from, so that we could preference sound and tone. She often read aloud in Swedish so I could hear the cadence and rhythm, the deep vowel sounds of the Swedish. In turn, I read my translations aloud in English as we refined them. Excerpts from *Atlantis* in my translation won the American-Scandinavian Foundation's Nadia Christensen Prize in Translation in 2018, following our residency.

"Desire is always a question," Silkeberg writes. The *desire* to see accurately, to report on what is seen and experienced (including what's experienced through others) must necessarily prompt *questions*. Questions about the nature of and impetus for what's observed, as well as questions about who is doing the observing. How do we exist, separate and different, but linked to others? What happens to human bonds in the face of war, migration, persistent malignant racial inequality? These poems offer us that the only answer to these questions is *struggle*, and that's why they stay with me (that, and their alluring sound and moments of cutting insight).

Working together with Silkeberg has changed my notion of what the role of a literary translator is – at least, I can speak for our case. I've been fortunate to learn more Swedish since meeting her, but I'm not fluent. We arrive at a translation together by talking through scenes in these very visual poems. She said once when trying to choose between phrasing: "I can't feel the difference in my language temperature" – and that's where I was able to be a sounding board. English is multiple, and versioning Marie's poems into a combination of her English and mine has created a deep literary friendship.

Tucson, Arizona, October 2020

---

[1] "Five ways to look at Malevich's Black Square," Tate, accessed September 7, 2020, https://www.tate.org.uk/art/artists/kazimir-malevich-1561/five-ways-look-malevichs-black-square.

Marie Silkeberg's Micro-Universes
Ranveig Kvinnsland

Marie Silkeberg is a prominent Swedish writer and translator of poetry and essays. In *Damascus, Atlantis*, we meet a selection of some of the most important poems from her two latest works, *Till Damaskus* (2014), a collaboration with the Syrian-Palestinian poet Ghayath Almadhoun, and *Atlantis* (2017). Both collections describe a world on the verge of collapse. Thematically, they are connected: *Till Damaskus* explores some of the consequences of and reactions to the preliminary phases of the civil war in Syria, while *Atlantis* explores, in addition to several other topics, some of the consequences of this war, and war itself as a phenomenon. These collections create their own micro-universes, helping readers gain new perspective on the chaos – as well as the connectedness – of our world. The form of Silkeberg's poems is derived from their political engagement. As US American poet Juliana Spahr once stated in an interview, "Politics are constantly shaping literary practices."[1]

Both *Till Damaskus* and *Atlantis* are complex, intense, and invigorating, and they are characterized by their vastness and length. But several immediate visual differences are apparent. The poems in *Atlantis* are long, with shorter lines – take "Cape Point," for instance, which is 40 pages long – but their pages are light, thanks to the space, the air, between the lines. This spacing demands that the reader adapt their reading pace to take the poems in. Many of the poems in *Atlantis* share in the US American long-poem discourse, particularly Lynn Keller's processual long poem, which often includes sociological, anthropological, and historical elements.[2] The geopolitical poetry of *Atlantis* can be read as commentary on worldwide conflict and struggle, and on the consequences of political action, crossing geographical, political, cultural-religious, and imaginative borders.

The poems in *Till Damaskus* are much more compact, visually and linguistically. Some of the lines are longer, while others consist of brief phrases that bleed into each other. These poems present the reader with the challenge of separating out their phrasal clusters. Many of the poems take the form of a square, as if to resemble the fuzzy screen of a broken TV. Silkeberg's squares depict the brutality of war, terror, fear, and the fight for survival.

The intensity and corresponding sense of exhaustion of both the square poems and the long poems can be understood as part of Silkeberg's poetics. She explores issues often covered in mainstream media – and any sense of normalcy in her micro-universes is time and again disturbed by the form in which the poems' issues, stories, and observations are conveyed. In the poems in this collection, brutality is extended either by actual duration and length, as in the long poems, or conveyed through the hoarseness of the square poems. The musicality, and especially the rhythm, of the two different poetic forms differentiates the reading process. From the extensive use of full stops in the square poems, to the wavy sequences of the long poems, these poems demand a patient reader.

The reader of Silkeberg's poems is placed in the present moment of the poems through the intimate density of the words and their evocative visual descriptions, but also through the poetic address. In the dense square poems, we meet an 'I' speaker, while the airy long poems are addressed to a 'you.' By combining *Till Damaskus* and *Atlantis*, the connection between the 'I; and the 'you' is intensified. Not only is the reader directly implicated, but a dialogue is created. Putting these poems in close connection to each other expands the narrative of both collections.

In my reading of this lyric address, I understand the 'you' of *Atlantis* triangularly: either as directed to an 'I' (the speaker themself), or to the reader, or to humankind more generally. In the poem "Bárðarbunga," 'you' travel around Iceland and reflect upon the power of nature. If read in connection to the age of Anthropocene, "Bárðarbunga" can be understood as a reflection on the actions of humankind on their surroundings. This poem describes a place on earth where the powers of nature overrule the powers of mankind. If we choose to read the 'you' as the lyric 'I,' the speaker can distance themself from humankind's invasion of nature, taking an apathetic relationship to their surroundings. The same apathy can be transferred to the third aforementioned reading of the 'you' – that is, humankind more generally – whose actions, lifestyles, and interests cause Earth pain. However, I find the second understanding of the 'you' most interesting, as it has the greatest impact on me as a reader. I am directly implicated in the actions described, as if I were the one executing them. And the poem does not provide me as a reader with an invitation that I can either accept or decline. As long as I accept the role of the reader, the actions are directly transferred to me. This type of lyric address forces me to rethink my actions, my choices.

Perhaps because I am implicated as a reader, the micro-universes presented by Silkeberg seem both foreign and familiar, in the sense of the late Danish writer Inger Christensen's 'condition of secrecy.' Christensen's work is central to Silkeberg's poetics – Silkeberg is Christensen's main translator into Swedish and has served as the editor of Christensen's unpublished archive. In an essay from *The Condition of Secrecy*, Christensen states that in our inner world, the world of thought and imagination, we can choose a word, for example 'rose,' and then we can close our eyes and a rose, with all its qualities, will appear in front of us. We know the size, the color, the smell – and just by naming the word, our inner mind will start to replay every important memory related to roses.[3] Following this idea, to write poetry is then to pick and choose between the immense limitlessness of languages. Languages offer the poet clues about the world, and the poet's choices of composition turn the inner world into the real world. Silkeberg's writing does not necessarily represent the world that we as readers think we know, but instead she presents, through her poetic style, a world to us for consideration.

Lastly, I would like to utilize my particular position as a reader of Silkeberg's poetry both in Swedish and in English translation to mention some of my experiences with this translation. Walter Benjamin once wrote that "true translation is transparent," and that the translation shall "shine even more fully on the original."[4] In making this selection from Silkeberg's latest works, Kelsi Vanada accomplishes just that. The translated poems provide a new perspective on both the aim and meaning of the originals, and the poems in this translation express the importance of the function of the poetic form, as has been described above.

The translation keeps the invigorating and characteristic style of Marie Silkeberg intact. To me, as a Scandinavian reader, the main difference between the original and the translation lies in Vanada's handling of Silkeberg's use of phrases, lines, and single words of English in the original Swedish. These moments underline the movement of globalization in which the poems exist. The poems are concerned with problems of global interest, they include meetings across borders, and the *lingua franca* – the English language – places these poems in a transnational and translingual tradition. For me, and for many others whose first language is not English, the English language is associated with power and knowledge: we learn it in order to take part in an international context. In these translations of Silkeberg's poems, the phrases which are in English in the original are sometimes marked by italics, and sometimes not marked at all. In doing so, the poems voice these utterances differently. The effect has to do with the voice of the speaker(s) relating the encounters these poems depict. The italics can be read as a whisper, rather than a voice of their own.

Reading poetry is like going on a conceptual treasure hunt. Your map is the poem itself, but the treasure will not reveal itself to you unless you are willing to commit to lifting every stone, to turning every word. Silkeberg's poems ask that readers give their attention without rushing; they demand a distinct engagement with temporality. This is poetry written "from the poet's need to identify her relationship to atrocities and injustice, the sources of her pain, fear, and anger, the meaning of her resistance."[5] Silkeberg's poetry, even as it creates its own universe, is a form of knowledge about our complex world.

Oslo, Norway, August 2020

[1] "Juliana Spahr Interview: Politics in a Poem," Louisiana Channel, June 23, 2015, https://www.youtube.com/watch?v=2uUvIBrMhmc.

[2] Lynn Keller, "The Twentieth-Century Long Poem," in *The Columbia History of American Poetry*, ed. Jay Parini (New York: Columbia University Press, 1993), 534-63.

[3] Inger Christensen, *The Condition of Secrecy*, trans. Susanna Nied (New York: New Directions Publishing, 2018).

[4] Walter Benjamin, "The Translator's Task," trans. Steven Rendall, *TTR* 10, no. 2 (1997), 151–165, https://doi.org/10.7202/037302ar.

[5] Edward Hirsch, *A Poet's Glossary* (Boston & New York: Houghton Mifflin Harcourt, 2014), 476-478.

Marie Silkeberg is a poet, translator, and poetry filmmaker living in Stockholm. She has published eight collections of poetry, including *23:23* (2006), *Material* (2010), and *Till Damaskus* (2014). *Atlantis* (2017) is her most recent book. She spent ten years as Professor in Creative Writing at Valand Academy at Gothenburg University and three years as HCA Academy Visiting Professor at the University of Southern Denmark. She has translated several books by the Danish poet Inger Christensen, as well as American poets such as Alice Notley, Susan Howe, Patti Smith, Rosmarie Waldrop, and Claudia Rankine. Together with different composers, filmmakers, and poets, she has made text and sound compositions and poetry films, the four most recent together with Ghayath Almadhoun. In 2015 she was a visiting writer at the International Writing Program in Iowa City, Iowa. She held a fellowship at the Vermont Studio Center in 2017, and a MacDowell Fellowship in New Hampshire in 2018.

www.mariesilkeberg.com

Kelsi Vanada holds an MFA in Poetry from the Iowa Writers' Workshop and an MFA in Literary Translation from the University of Iowa. She translates from Spanish and collaboratively from Swedish. Her previous translations include Sergio Espinosa's *Into Muteness* (Veliz Books, 2020) and Berta García Faet's *The Eligible Age* (Song Bridge Press, 2018), and she is the author of the poetry chapbook *Rare Earth* (Finishing Line Press, 2020). Since July 2018, Kelsi has worked as the Program Manager of the American Literary Translators Association (ALTA) in Tucson, Arizona.

www.kelsi-vanada.com

Ranveig Kvinnsland is studying Norwegian literature at the University of Oslo, currently focusing on contemporary Scandinavian poetry. It is she who introduced the work of Silkeberg to Terra Nova Press, the American publisher.